THE *Mind,* *Heart,* AND *Soul* OF DEPRESSION

YOUR GUIDED JOURNAL FOR EMOTIONAL HEALING AND GETTING TO THE TRUTH OF THE MATTER

CATHY L. REIMERS PH.D.

BALBOA.
PRESS

A DIVISION OF HAY HOUSE

Cover design- Elyse Jennings
Graphics illustrator- Phil Juliano

Balboa Press books may be ordered through booksellers or by contacting:

Balboa Press
A Division of Hay House
1663 Liberty Drive
Bloomington, IN 47403
www.balboapress.com
1 (877) 407-4847

Because of the dynamic nature of the Internet, any web addresses or links contained in this book may have changed since publication and may no longer be valid. The views expressed in this work are solely those of the author and do not necessarily reflect the views of the publisher, and the publisher hereby disclaims any responsibility for them.

The author of this book does not dispense medical advice or prescribe the use of any technique as a form of treatment for physical, emotional, or medical problems without the advice of a physician, either directly or indirectly. The intent of the author is only to offer information of a general nature to help you in your quest for emotional and spiritual well-being. In the event you use any of the information in this book for yourself, which is your constitutional right, the author and the publisher assume no responsibility for your actions.

Any people depicted in stock imagery provided by Thinkstock are models,
and such images are being used for illustrative purposes only.
Certain stock imagery © Thinkstock.

Print information available on the last page.

ISBN: 978-1-5043-6422-5 (sc)
ISBN: 978-1-5043-6427-0 (e)

Library of Congress Control Number: 2016912954

Balboa Press rev. date: 08/29/2016

DEDICATION

This book is for anyone who has suffered from depression but believes that healing is possible by getting to the *Truth* of the *Matter* of our *Mind, Heart* and *Soul.*

ACKNOWLEDGMENTS

I owe a debt of gratitude to some people who have contributed to this book in many ways.

First, I want to thank my daughter, Emilie, who encouraged me to "follow my passion" in starting this mental health series.

Very special thanks to my daughter-in-law, Elyse, who designed a book cover that is a true inspiration.

Much appreciation to my editor, Cathi Laughlin, who gave me fortitude, endurance and patience. I want to thank Linda Levinson, my best friend and Diana Hanselka, my sister, who are a beacon of light and hope, and who guided me through the tough times.

And last, but not least, a very special thanks to my dog Honey, who always licks the tears from my cheeks when I'm navigating life's challenges.

****

During the course of publishing this book, my 92-year-old mother, endearingly referred to as Mimi, suffered a major stroke. She was not expected to recover. The trauma left me numb, exhausted and hopeless.

I've been a therapist for many years, and suddenly, I found myself needing to practice what I preach. I learned that I had to reach for help, and thankfully, many people were there for me. I also found that browsing through this book and its illustrations made me smile. I hope this book will inspire other people who are also having a difficult time.

My family and I are deeply grateful for the assistance and support given to us from the members of the Chesterfield Baptist Church in Chesterfield, New Jersey. We are also exceedingly appreciative to the entire medical and professional staffs at the Masonic Home of New Jersey in Burlington, New Jersey.

Both organizations provided unconditional acts of love, which opened up my heart and reenergized my mind and soul again, and subsequently, allowed me to continue my life's work of helping and healing others. For that, I am deeply grateful.

CONTENTS

INTRODUCTION

Do you think you are depressed? If so, reading and completing the written exercises in this journal can help you expand your mind, heal your heart, and reach into the depths of your soul.

Depression is a common but serious illness that can become a chronic condition.

It's no secret that, in our stressed society, more and more Americans are living with major depressive disorder (MDD).

What is depression?

Severe depression can be characterized by intense and prolonged sadness, loss of pleasure and concentration, low energy, feelings of worthlessness, and eating and sleep disturbances. If depression worsens, suicidal ideation or homicidal acts can occur.

Who might be depressed? Old men, young women, preschoolers, teens, victims of abuse, military veterans, athletes, truck drivers, and so on. Anyone can suffer from MDD.

Depression by the Numbers

- Nearly 7 percent of adults (16 million) experience depression, according to a report from the National Alliance on Mental Health.
- Women are almost 70 percent more likely than men to experience depression during their lifetimes.
- MDD is the leading cause of disability in the US for persons aged 15–44, according to the Center for Disease Control's report.
- Persons aged 19–24 report depressive symptoms more than other age groups.

MDD is often misconstrued, minimized, and even mocked by the people the sufferer loves most. To make matters worse, people diagnosed with any mental health disorder often feel a great deal of guilt. It's a social stigma that I refer to as "hiding under the cloak of shame."

Family members, coworkers, supervisors, friends, and partners often make comments to people suffering from depression, such as, "You're just depressed," or "Get over it," or "Just get out of bed." They might say, "You'll feel better if you go to the gym," or "It's menopause, and this happens," or "Go to work and get your mind off it."

Being misunderstood and trivialized can lead one to experience more intense feelings of inadequacy, loneliness, helplessness, and rejection. Then there is the constant challenge of trying to behave normally among others, which can lead us to suffer more internal pain. This quiet suffering can be exhausting and cause deeper emotional wounds that become rooted in our psyches, in our hearts, and even in the depths of our souls.

Depression is a lonely disease. At times we isolate ourselves and become socially invisible when we should be reaching out to others who do care about us. In an era where our "friends" on Facebook see where we dine, what we wear, and how we travel, we often confuse the intimacy of sharing our statuses on social media with the authenticity of sharing our real selves with others.

Often we look for unhealthy ways to soothe the pain. Mental illness is often disguised by substance addiction, gambling, or domestic violence and may not be acknowledged until it's too late. The tragic deaths of some celebrities (Philip Seymour Hoffman, Amy Winehouse, Whitney Houston, and her daughter Bobbi Kristina Brown) show that depression doesn't discriminate. Depression doesn't care how wealthy, smart, or successful you are.

Another reality is that nowadays the doctor-patient relationship is strained. Many primary care physicians and some others in the medical field have preconceived notions, negative biases, and limited understanding of how MDD affects a person's life.

They may identify it only as a physical problem caused by an imbalance of neurotransmitters, although it can be much more than that. In response, they prescribe medicine as a primary treatment and only refer the patient to the mental health community if the patient is deemed "too difficult."

Other doctors appear uninterested in the patient's problems. Some medical professionals have little time to listen to the patient because of the pressures of insurance company mandates.

Furthermore, the range of therapies and the number of sessions that mental health providers can provide are often limited by rules governed by insurance companies. Consequently, many therapists will prematurely conclude their services with patients and refer them back to general practitioners, other psychologists, or psychiatrists for further medical treatment. Complicating matters, there are not enough mental health practitioners available, causing some health care workers to be overburdened and unable to accept new patients who need help.

Just imagine how frustrating it can be for a patient who is dealing with constant depression to be stuck in the labyrinth of bureaucracy. These obstacles can make a patient feel dehumanized and even more hopeless.

With these roadblocks in our path to authentic mental health, what can we do to help us understand ourselves and gain the clarity to get well?

1. Why Write in a Journal?

Writing in a journal allows you to begin the process of finding the core of *you*. It is a journey of self-discovery. You may choose to open doors that you never considered. You may elect to travel down paths that are uncertain. You may find a new meaning and purpose for your life. Whatever you uncover is up to you.

If true healing is to take place, the patient must commit to a journey of deep self-inquiry and self-examination. For the past twenty-five years that I have been a practicing psychologist, I've discovered that those answers are often found if you listen to your inner voice. I have also discovered that writing in a journal can be a perfect way to express your thoughts, feelings, and views while finding realistic solutions.

When you are upset, you might repeat negative messages and thoughts to yourself. Journaling can help you break out of these mood slumps and free yourself from negative internal voices.

It can help you peel back layers of fear and pain. Fear becomes the roadblock, impeding our judgment and reasoning; pain becomes the sinkhole, swallowing our energy, life, and soul.

This journal can guide you to understand your particular situation and help you discover any impasses that are blocking positive feelings and inhibiting healing. When you live your truths, you end up loving your life, and depression fades.

Research shows that journaling helps organize thoughts, soothes hurtful feelings, and encourages creativity so that the process of healing can begin.

This journal is not a replacement for psychotherapy, medications, and/or other treatments for depression. The goal of this journal is to help you educate yourself about depression, express your innermost thoughts and feelings, and eventually establish a path toward emotional healing.

2. Carrie and Her Horses

Depression can begin at a young age and continue throughout a person's life.

Young people often act out signs of depression with anger, rage, extreme irritability, or despondency. These behaviors are often misidentified as normal moodiness and can be overlooked and forgotten.

Many people experience depression, but it can be a serious illness when it becomes persistent and long-term.

Growing up, Carrie lived on a horse farm, and the horses were her life's joy. She sometimes daydreamed of the day when she might be able to tame a wild stallion. Soon Carrie became a competitive equestrian, winning more blue ribbons and trophies than her shelves could hold.

Throughout her teens, she grew inward and stopped socializing with her friends. By age eighteen, she was spending most of her time in her room and neglecting to do her chores, such as grooming her horses. She also stopped competing in horse shows.

Initially, her parents believed Carrie's ambivalence and mood swings were typical adolescent behavior. As time passed, her father became more frustrated and called her *lazy*. "Just get over it!" he screamed.

Her mother felt empathy for Carrie's anguish, but she was unaware of how to help her daughter.

"Why don't you go running with me?" she suggested. "If you get a little exercise, you'll feel better."

Soon Carrie grew tired of dealing with her parents and closed the blinds so she didn't have to look at the horses. All she wanted to do was sleep and dream of wild stallions, wishing she was one of them.

Carrie's situation with her parents was typical. Her depression was misunderstood, minimized, and derided by the people who loved her.

3. JOURNALING WILL OPEN YOUR MIND

This handbook is divided into ten parts to help you understand the causes of your depression. You will learn that there are many symptoms and sources of your depression.

The journal begins with the definition and the breakdown of MDD. Other sections outline the links between the brain's chemistry and depression; effects of traumatic experiences; risks of depression; impact of family and other relationships; when to seek help; treatment options; support systems, including national organizations; and, ultimately, the lessons of depression.

To help you understand further, each topic is followed by short, sometimes whimsical stories that illustrate larger, meaningful lessons. They are followed by questions for you to reflect upon and get to the truth of the matter.

Throughout the journal, the questions will help you to explore your upbringing; relationships with family, friends, and coworkers; your education; career choices; any traumatic experiences; and any innate or biological qualities that contribute to your behavior.

In my practice, people tell me that when they write about themselves and their experiences, their moods improve, their symptoms of depression decrease, and they begin to feel better overall. Expressive writing gets to the heart of the matter.

I encourage you to complete as many questions as you can. If you become stuck answering any question, skip it and go on to the next one. You can always go back and answer it later.

Throughout the journal, I will introduce traditional methods to aid in managing or reducing symptoms of depression, such as cognitive, insight-oriented, and family-systems therapies.

Creativity is another approach that aids in the treatment of depression. On some pages of the journal, you will be asked to draw. Your creative expressions can unconsciously uncover answers buried deep within you.

A theme throughout the journal is nature. Studies show that connecting to nature can elevate your physical well-being and mental health. It is my hope that, by imagining the powerful elements of earth, you will feel the heartbeat of your soul.

Those of us who have pets understand the concept of unconditional love and how the relationship between owners and pets can improve our hearts, both physically and emotionally. I believe that we can learn much from interacting with our pets, who connect with us in ways that humans may not.

Mindfulness, a method introduced into the field of psychology in recent years, can also be very helpful in treating depression. Although it seems simple, mindfulness is not always easy because it goes against how we normally think.

Mindfulness is paying attention to something in the present without judgment. Instead of thinking about your business trip next week, you remain aware of the orange juice that's been placed in front of you. You comprehend its orange color. You savor its sweet smell. As you swallow the juice, you feel its cool sensation.

My hope is that by writing in this journal, you will begin to think more positively, break through barriers, build confidence, and accept yourself without feeling guilty, embarrassed, or ashamed.

Ultimately, if you identify with five MDD symptoms in this book, you may be clinically depressed, and you should seek professional treatment.

How to Begin Your Journal Journey

Step one: Find a quiet, comfortable setting. It can be a favorite spot in your home or outside in nature. Free yourself from all distractions. Clear your mind, take a deep breath, and exhale slowly. This journey requires focus as you enter those places where you may have feared to go.

Step two: Feel free to write over or outside the images or anywhere else on the journal pages. Writing without boundaries allows your creative nature to be expressed, reflecting the beauty dwelling within you.

Step three: Some questions may be easy to answer; others may appear difficult. Pay particular attention to those questions that are difficult for you to answer. They may lead you to your greatest insights in conquering problems. Growth comes from struggle. Struggle leads to increased strength, which leads to truth. By becoming more honest with yourself, you will cultivate a perfect peace as you start to unravel your depression.

PART I. SYMPTOMS OF DEPRESSION

1. MY SADNESS

When you experience a major depressive episode, you might feel there is no bottom.

Bottomless Pit of Depression

Allan was very much in love with his girlfriend. It was the first time he had been in a relationship.

After a year, Allan's girlfriend told him that things weren't working out, and she broke up with him. Months later he still felt depressed, as if a great weight pulled him down all day.

What weighs upon you that is so heavy?

On the rocks, write down any conflicts, burdens, obligations, or stressors that weigh you down. If you can't identify where the heaviness comes from, put a question mark on the rock.

Many burdens are only as heavy as you make them. Think of a stressor. Have you made it bigger and weightier than it needs to be?

Does your resistance to the conflict make it easier or harder to lift?

Identify a problem and accept it. See what happens.

2. MY LOSS OF INTEREST

Sometimes we lose interest in activities and pursuits that we have enjoyed for prolonged periods. This could be a sign that we're depressed.

Where Did My Little Dog Go?

We're all familiar with this rhyming song for children: "Oh where, oh where has my little dog gone? Oh where, oh where can he be?"

Jackie's dog has run away because Jackie stopped caring for her. Imagine that your little dog ran away because you also stopped caring for him. You find him, and you pull him close to your heart.

Write about any daily activities that you have stopped doing.

What will make you start doing them again?

Make a list of any new activities that you would like to try.

3. My Restlessness

Many people associate depression with inactivity, which may be true for numerous people. Others face depression by keeping busy. As anxiety builds, they work longer hours, schedule countless social events, or perform scores of home-improvement projects. To an observer, their lives may seem balanced, but an unsuspected downward spiral into depression can occur.

Busy as a Beaver

Benny the beaver was a hardworking multi-tasker. He spent his days constructing an elaborate habitat. Yet when he built his dams, Benny gnawed and destroyed a multitude of trees. His dams also modified the normal flow of rivers and streams and caused flooding.

Like Benny's, your busyness may cause more harm than good.

Are you too busy?

What are you busy doing?

Are you covering up your feelings by being absorbed in projects?

What do you need to uncover? Do you need to dig deeper?

In the speech balloon, write down some ways to help you relax.

4. My Moodiness

Sometimes life makes us irritated. There's an accident on the interstate that makes you an hour late for an office meeting. A neighbor's dog digs up the tulips you planted in your yard. Sometimes we refuse to accept situations that are beyond our control. That irritability can foster feelings of negativity, which is how depression can be manifested. Often we are not aware of how it affects others.

Irritable Warrior

Basil was a brave warrior. But he was always negative and irritable. The others in his legion didn't want to be around him. He constantly complained and put others down. Nothing was to his liking. His fellow warriors grew weary of his complaints and overall negativity.

One morning Basil awakened and realized that his legion had moved on and left him behind. Basil had no one to grumble to, grouse about, or criticize.

All alone, he questioned himself. Surely he was more than a complainer. Or was he? He fell to his knees and sobbed. Suddenly he felt a little hand on his shoulder.

Finish the story.

What does the child say to the warrior?

What does the warrior say?

How does the warrior feel?

Give this warrior a gift. Write a description of the gift that will help the warrior.

5. MY HOPELESSNESS

Feelings of hopelessness are often at the core of depression, and those feelings can be hard to escape, no matter how hard you try. Hopelessness comes from experiencing total abandonment, oppression, terminal illness, death, failure in a relationship or job, and other hardships. Sometimes we just feel tortured by life.

Dungeon of Despair

Simon knew that his beheading was scheduled for the next morning. His swollen and bruised body, curled in a fetal position, pulsed with pain from the beatings. Worse were the deeper wounds of mental anguish he was suffering from the cruel interrogations.

"Death might be a welcome comfort," he thought to himself. Lying in the dark, he faded in and out of consciousness. Suddenly he heard something. He looked toward the steel door, and a bright light blinded him. He'd heard people talk about seeing beams of light during near-death experiences. Yet he could feel his arms and legs. Was someone coming, or was he dead?

In this dire situation, should Simon give up hope?

Describe how he might be saved.

How can he keep his hope alive?

What are you feeling hopeless about in your life?

How do you get out of your own dungeon of despair?

Who helps you do this?

6. MY SLEEP

Major depression can cause sleep problems. Many depressives sleep all the time; others have trouble sleeping at all. Sometimes you may feel like a zombie, numb and lifeless, and completely insensitive to the world around you.

Zombie Daddy and Mommy

Each night Gus tried to fall asleep after reading to his two daughters, but he only tossed and turned. His eyes were always bloodshot, with deep, dark circles beneath them. Ironically, his wife Clare wanted to sleep all the time. The couple's girls called their parents Zombie Daddy and Zombie Mommy.

Describe your sleep patterns. What time do you fall asleep?

Do you have trouble falling asleep?

Do you have trouble staying asleep?

Have you resorted to certain rituals, such as watching TV or using your laptop?

What time do you wake?

Are there days that you don't sleep?

How many hours do you normally sleep?

Are there days that you want to sleep all the time?

When you don't sleep enough, how does it make you feel?

Do you ever sleep more than ten hours?

Does it affect your outlook?

7. MY APPETITE

When you're struggling with depression, your eating habits often change. Depression often causes a lack of appetite and can also trigger "emotional hunger"—eating to feel better.

At the core of eating problems are feelings of shame, guilt, and/or worthlessness. Feeling powerless over your emotions might make you feel powerless over food.

Twin Torment

Identical twins Eve and Zoe were happy thirteen-year-olds. Then their mother died of cancer. Their father, grief-stricken over the loss of his wife, withdrew into his own depression, barely speaking to them.

As the months passed, the twins became more desperate. Eve stopped eating, but Zoe ate everything, sometimes finishing her sister's meals. Eve lost weight while Zoe added many pounds.

Anxiety and depression overwhelmed the girls. While Eve's sad emotions provoked a loss of appetite, Zoe coped with her negative feelings by overeating.

Do you lose your appetite when you are upset?

For what are you emotionally starved?

When you're depressed, do you binge on food or alcohol?

How does bingeing make you feel afterward?

Identify times when you gained weight because you were depressed.

Try to identify the seeds of this behavior.

8. MY CONCENTRATION

When you experience a depressive episode, concentration is greatly diminished, affecting problem solving, memory, and focus.

Arrow's Point

Naomi was the best female archer, successfully hunting squirrels, rabbits, and foxes. Her excellent skills pleased the wicked queen, who gave her a stone house, gilded clothing, and gold coins.

Her brother Daniel, who was a few years older, was also a revered archer. He had taught Naomi to hunt.

One day Daniel didn't return from a hunting expedition. Naomi became very sad and unable to hunt the easiest prey. The queen threatened to cast her into the dungeon. Naomi begged for one last chance. The queen obliged, ordering Naomi to shoot an apple upon the head of the queen's favorite nobleman. Naomi concentrated and slowly pulled back the bow's string.

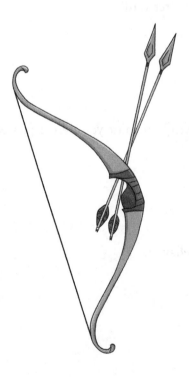

Does Naomi hit the apple?

Why or why not?

Finish the story.

Are there times when you have difficulty concentrating?

Does this occur when you are upset?

What are the consequences of being distracted?

9. My Body Aches

Although depression is a mental disorder, it can affect you physically, causing changes throughout your body. Unexpressed feelings of anger, loneliness, frustration, and hurt often lead to physical ailments such as muscle pain, chronic body aches, and headaches.

Puzzling Pain

Four-year-old George lived with his wealthy parents in a mansion. Butlers, housekeepers, and drivers served his every whim. But his parents paid little attention to him.

As time went by, George experienced chronic body aches and was very tired almost every day. His parents hired the best doctors, who helped to ease his symptoms. But they couldn't find a cause for his aches.

Then George's parents hired a nanny to care for him. George loved the nanny, who played board games with him, taught him to read, and took him to the park. George's health improved, and his body aches began to disappear.

Have you noticed any illnesses, aches, or pains when you feel stressed or sad?

Explain the circumstances.

Notice what part of your body repeatedly holds your emotional pain. Where is it?

Take your hand and place it over any part of your body that hurts. Feel the energy from your hand. Allow your own energy to heal you.

10. MY GUILT

Guilt results from thinking that one has done something bad, which often results in becoming depressed. Sometimes we can identify the cause of the guilt, but not always. Sometimes we carry someone else's guilt without being aware of how we're actually feeling.

Just Around the Corner

Thirteen-year-old Tanya walked her five-year-old brother Owen to school every day. Crossing a busy intersection one morning, Tanya let go of her brother's hand to look at the text just sent by her friend. Suddenly a car turned the corner, hitting and killing Owen, who had walked in front of Tanya.

For years Tanya felt guilty about not holding her brother's hand, something she had done every time she walked him to school.

Her mother felt guilty for giving Tanya the responsibility of supervising Owen every day. Her father felt guilty that his wife had needed to go back to work after he had lost his job. Joanie, Tanya's sister, who was eighteen months old at the time of the accident, grew up carrying a lot of guilt and shame, having absorbed the negative emotions from her family members throughout the years.

Identify events that you feel guilty about and make a list of them.

Notice how many you have. Are you carrying anyone else's guilt? Explain.

Guilt is a chosen response. Choose to replace guilt with other feelings. What feelings come to mind?

Write a letter of apology to yourself.

11. MY ANXIETY

Anxiety is worry or apprehension concerning past events. The sufferer may keep thinking, "I should have done that. Why did this have to happen?"

Anxiety may also take the form of fear of the future: "What if this happens?"

Anxiety is like hanging from a skyscraper. Depression feels like you've already fallen and hit bottom. Anxiety can drive a depressive episode. Give someone enough worries, and depression will slip into a person's psyche.

Prison of the Mind

Martha found herself in prison. She didn't know how she got there. She was alone. She worried about her past. What had she done wrong?

Neurotic thoughts flooded her mind. Was she a good worker? Did she pay the electric bill? What was that bump on her nose? What did her parents think about her being in prison? Would her boyfriend wait for her?

She paced back and forth, finally accepting her situation. As her mind became quiet, she leaned against the door. Surprisingly, it swung open—as Martha awoke from a dream.

Only then did she realize that her anxiety had been keeping her a prisoner for years.

Are you a prisoner of your anxiety?

On the wall, write all your main worries. Tally up the years that you have worried.

What are the keys to unlock your worries?

Who can help you if the keys get jammed?

PART II. CHEMISTRY

1. My Brain

MDD can be biological, which often explains the deep sadness and sometimes suicidal thoughts that might occur for no apparent reason. The chemicals in our brains affect the way we think, act, and feel.

Having It All

Veronica was promoted to the management position that she'd wanted all along. She was living in a modern Manhattan apartment and was dating the person of her dreams. Finally her life was where she wanted it to be.

But as she lay awake before getting ready for work, a deep sadness fell upon her. She almost couldn't move her legs to the floor. She immediately thought about her mom. When Veronica was growing up, her mother spent many days lying in a darkened bedroom.

On the page, compare the flasks. Are there any behaviors that are similar to the traits of your biological parents? On the flask marked *Mom,* write the words that describe the behaviors and emotions of your biological mom. Do the same on the flasks marked *Dad* and *Essence of Me.* On the last flask, the one marked *New and Improved,* write any new traits you want for yourself.

PART III. TRAUMATIC EXPERIENCES

1. My Accident

Studies indicate that people who experience horrific or traumatic events show higher rates of depression and often suffer for years.

Crashed Soul

Sarah and her parents were on their way to sunny Puerto Rico when one of the plane's engines exploded, causing it to crash right before the runway. Sarah and five other passengers survived. Her parents perished. For years Sarah was angry, and then she became depressed. She questioned her existence and continually relived the accident.

Growing up, Sarah had played the guitar. She and her parents, who were artists, would play together on Sunday nights. Sarah would accompany her mother, who played the piano, while Sarah's father sang.

After much prodding from a friend, Sarah began to take guitar lessons again. Sarah's instructor suggested that she play at a senior home. Sarah agreed.

Each week Sarah was touched by the residents as they sang to her music. Each time she played, she felt her parents' presence. Over time, she rebuilt her life.

Do you have a traumatic life event that never leaves you and causes you to be depressed?

When you think about it, identify your mood and notice how your body feels.

How can you let your trauma go and accept it?

Will helping others fill the hole?

2. MY CHILD ABUSE

Child abuse can be physical, sexual, or emotional. It's no secret that a child who is abused may be more likely to abuse others when he or she becomes an adult. Other victims find themselves in relationships where they are abused over and over again.

As a result, generational child abuse spawns ongoing cycles of depression.

Devoured by the Shadow

Mindy the mouse wandered deep inside a den while searching for food. As she tried to leave, a huge shadow hovered overhead. The shadow climbed on Mindy, who found herself getting weaker. She couldn't fight, and she became paralyzed with fear.

Finish the story.

Were you ever the victim of physical or sexual abuse?

Who was in your den/home?

Draw a brick wall. Letting go of the pain or "blocks" from abuse can be hard. Take one block out of the wall each day until the wall is removed.

How do you feel now that the wall is down?

Who or what do you need to defend against? If you still feel that you need to defend yourself, then you probably still have a block that needs to be removed.

With whom can you share your story?

Rewrite the story. Describe yourself acting with courage and determination. Such a story can be healing.

Healing depends on the courage to face your truth and forgive yourself and perhaps even the perpetrator, keeping in mind that even perpetrators can be victims.

PART IV. RISKS OF DEPRESSION

1. MY SELF-DESTRUCTION

Suicidal thoughts or suicide attempts are risks of depression. Those risks frequently stem from suffering that comes from sleeplessness and illness, adverse reactions to medication, prolonged depression, trauma, and intense stress. Depression can make you feel as though you've entered an arctic cave of darkness and that there is no way out.

Arctic Cave

A year after his longtime partner had slid to his death while the couple were hiking, Henry traveled back to the Canadian arctic region. The region had been a favorite hiking destination for them. Since losing his partner, Henry had been filled with sorrow and depression.

An unexpected blizzard made it impossible for Henry to see the trail. He trudged to a barely visible cave and collapsed within its dark, cold walls. As the storm continued throughout the freezing night, Henry thought how easy it would be to end his own life in the cave. He felt so tired of living.

When he awoke, he noticed a shiny object on the ground. He focused his flashlight and saw that it was a crystal rock. He saw his reflection. He looked closer and saw the images of his and his partner's children.

The storm ended, and Henry exited the cave, carrying the crystal close to his heart. He didn't know which way to go. Mountains of snow covered the land. Encouraged by his children's faces, though, Henry moved forward.

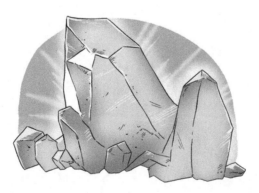

Draw images of yourself and your loved ones in the crystal. Imagine placing the crystal near your heart.

PART V. FAMILY

1. My Early Environment

Although depression can be inherited and body chemistry can impact your feelings, both your depression and your feelings can be influenced by your surroundings and your childhood environment.

The genesis of depression can be traced back to unresolved family conflicts and toxic family environments. This is why so much attention is given to understanding your past relationships with your family. Feeling trapped in family conflict might prevent healing.

Depression can worsen if a child doesn't form a proper attachment or bond with a caregiver or if the child isn't a priority in the caregiver's life. When a child is raised by people with explosive temperaments or by someone who is chronically depressed, the child is more prone to depression and anxiety.

Excavating unresolved anger, conflict, or friction is necessary for true healing to occur.

Describe your family while you were growing up. Draw stick figures representing you and your family members in the house. Draw your family members with expressions (happy, sad, angry, neutral) on their faces. If your parents were divorced, do the same thing in the other house.

Shackled to Surroundings

Marcus was an angry and depressed teenager. In his dark bedroom, he spent long hours playing video games and avoiding his unhappy father. His father grew up with abusive parents who had told him that he was a failure. He perpetuated the abuse cycle, yelling repeatedly at Marcus, his sister, and their mother.

His mother pleaded daily with Marcus to go to school. She pleaded with him to shower. She routinely placed his meals outside his room.

When his father died suddenly in a car accident, Marcus still didn't come out of his room. He didn't express any emotions, sad or happy.

What was your room like?

What feelings come to mind?

Why?

Write about an ideal family life. What did you need and want but not receive from your family?

How can you get these needs and wants fulfilled now?

From whom?

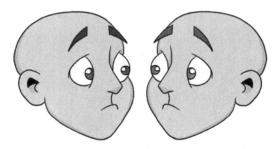

Describe your relationships with your mother, your father, or the people who raised you. Were those relationships close, fragile, contentious, distant, or nonexistent?

Did you ever feel abandoned by those who took care of you? Explain.

Were you a priority in their lives?

Are you a priority now?

Did those who cared for you have symptoms of depression?

Did they know that you suffered from depression, either in your youth or as an adult?

How did they handle your depression?

If they didn't know about your depression, what was that like for you?

What prevents you from letting these family members or caregivers know about your depression now?

2. MY FAMILY SECRETS

Even though we live in an age of less privacy, secrets still endure, especially in families. Secrets surrounding physical or sexual abuse, extramarital affairs, divorce, serious health issues, financial problems, or death can be the roots of depression.

Locked in the Mind

Jenna's parents had never had a healthy relationship, often fighting about money. They had married right after high school, when her mother found out she was pregnant with Jenna. Shortly after Jenna turned ten, her father died.

About a year later, Jenna's mom, who feared being alone, married a man she barely knew after meeting him in a bar.

One day Jenna's stepfather hugged her. It didn't feel right. Eventually her stepfather committed acts of sexual abuse. These encounters occurred whenever Jenna and her stepfather were alone. Jenna eventually went to live with her grandmother.

Jenna is now married and the mother of three children. She has never told anyone about her stepfather. She carries the secret around all the time.

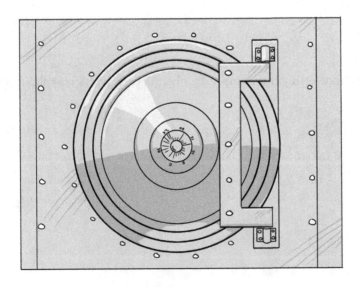

Do you carry secrets with you?

Were there secrets in your family? Place them in the vault.

Give the combination to someone you trust. Who can you trust in your life?

Now open the vault and tell the secret. Does telling your family secret to someone you trust help ease some of the depression?

3. MY FAMILY SHAME

Shame is feeling unwanted, worthless, and somehow not good enough. We learn shame while growing up, and it is often passed from one generation to the next.

Shame can be the worst possible emotion that you feel about yourself. In moments of shame, you feel that you are not accepted by your family and friends and are unfit to live in your community.

Hiding under the Cloak of Shame

Colton was a scribe who hid under his cloak. He never wanted to show his face. The king said, "Why do you hide from me, scribe?"

Colton replied, "My family is poor. My mom is a mad witch. My father has only one leg to stand upon. And, worst of all, I only have one eye."

The king thought a moment and said, "Ah, but the courage it took to tell me all this shows great strength. One good eye that can see the truth is better than two perfect eyes that are blind to it."

Do you feel or have you felt shame?

What is under your cloak?

Know and understand that shame is not your fault. Do you still carry shame around today?

How has family shame impacted your depression?

Are there other family members who feel or have felt shame?

4. MY SELF-IMAGE

When you have high self-worth or self-esteem, you feel deserving of respect. Low self-worth or self-esteem can cause us to feel negatively about ourselves and can be a consequence of depression.

Fading Flower

Carly and her mother were shopping at the mall. Carly, who was six, didn't want to be there and started having a tantrum. She wanted her mother's attention—even negative attention. Her mother became angry, and they left the mall.

As they approached their car, Carly saw a withered rose on the street. Captivated by its pink color, she picked it up and showed it to her mother, who was still reeling from Carly's tantrum.

Her mother slapped it out of her daughter's hand. "Throw that away! It's a dirty flower!"

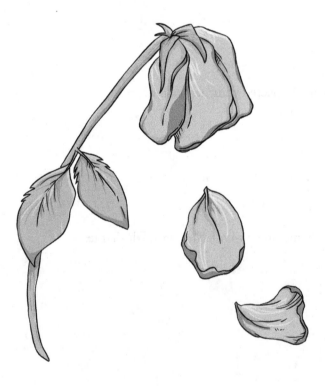

Be the mother. What feelings does she express?

Is she aware of her residual anger?

Be the girl. In the flower, describe the girl's reaction.

What does the flower symbolize in your life?

5. My Family Boundaries

Enmeshed families, or families that have no emotional boundaries, ultimately make children feel that they are not free to have their own identities and feelings. When children don't have their own voices, they feel less confident, more afraid, and too dependent upon parents or caregivers. The children will harbor resentment, which turns into depression.

Best Friends Forever

Bonnie and her daughter, Sophie, told people they were best friends. Bonnie never disciplined Sophie, leaving the job to Sophie's father. The two shared clothes and food and went on vacations together. Bonnie always told Sophie what to do, even choosing Sophie's college and career paths.

At her first job, Sophie met a man and fell madly in love. Bonnie didn't like him. "But Mom, I plan to marry him," Sophie told her mother.

Bonnie replied, "He's not good enough for you, honey. I will pick out someone who will be just right for you. I'm your best friend, remember? I won't steer you wrong."

What is wrong with Sophie's relationship with her mother?

Describe the boundaries you had with your parent or caregiver. Were they firm, loose, or nonexistent?

Growing up, did your family have emotional boundaries?

Did you ever feel that you didn't have a voice within the family unit?

Did you have your own voice, or did they speak for you—as well as feel for you?

What conflicts did you have with them?

Do you have those same conflicts in your personal relationships now?

Did your parents or caregiver really know you?

What prevents you from letting them know you now?

6. MY CONTROLLING FAMILY

Family members who feel that their lives are out of control often exhibit depression. Family members can be out of control in many ways and act out by manipulating, arguing, overspending, overeating, overworking, abusing drugs or alcohol, or overextending their time with too many activities and obligations.

Rule of the Throne

The king adored his daughter, Princess Rosetta, and allowed her to rule the realm. His wife, Queen Rosalind, was very jealous of her daughter and attempted to gain more favor with the king, often exaggerating the slightest misdeeds of the princess. The queen and the princess bickered constantly.

"This fighting must stop—or one of you will be banished from the kingdom!" the king told them.

When the fighting continued, the king had them play a game. It would show him to be a fair man. It also would reveal who had the most courage, the most important trait in the person who would rule his kingdom.

"The game is called *The Rule of the Throne*," he said. "Pick a hand. One contains a ruby, and one does not. If you pick the ruby, you will rule the kingdom."

Finish the story.

Did anyone decline the contest?

Who got the ruby?

Who was the king, queen, princess, or prince in your family?

Manipulation is a form of control. Were there members of your family who manipulated others?

Do you manipulate others?

In what ways?

What can you do to help yourself?

7. MY TRIGGERS

Emotional triggers are incidences from your past that penetrate your psyche as you grow up. As an adult, they cause you to relive experiences and the feelings associated with them.

Shattered Self

Emma's father was a carpenter who consumed shots of whiskey more numerous than the nails he hammered into lumber. Months would pass when he wouldn't work. The family struggled to pay their bills and buy food. During these spells, Emma's mother would yell, and her father would respond by throwing dishes and punching holes in the walls.

Whenever Emma hears the crash of something breaking or hears someone yelling, she breaks into a sweat; her heart starts beating rapidly.

What triggers set off your emotions?

Can you trace them to family members or others in your past?

Indicate if alcohol or any drugs, such as painkillers, were involved.

List the triggers or circumstances that cause these emotions.

8. MY EMOTIONAL MESSAGES I CARRY

As you grew into an adult, a family member's pain might have manifested as your own pain. That's why it's important to identify any negative messages that your family members carry.

Burdened with Messages

Jeff graduated college with a degree in microbiology. This was a tremendous achievement for Jeff, who had been diagnosed with learning problems as a child.

But Jeff can't bring himself to send out résumés. Sometimes he hears his father's cruel voice, in which he ridiculed Jeff as a child: "There's nothing wrong with you. You're just lazy. You'll never amount to anything."

What negative messages did you get from family members?

Write the messages on the letters or packages.

These messages sometimes shift into our current relationships. What messages do you carry?

What is the most important issue that people need to learn about you when you are having a depressive episode?

What should they do when you are in an episode?

Now write a letter to them. If you choose not to send it, put it in this imaginary bottle and send it out to sea.

9. MY SIBLINGS

Siblings who do not suffer from depression sometimes suffer emotionally in other ways. They might dwell in the shadow of a family member who suffers from depression.

The Lamb and the Bear

Liddy, who was seven, didn't seem like the kind of child who would make her parents worry. When Liddy was a baby, her parents bragged about her docile personality, referring to her as their little lamb.

Liddy became a stellar student and was always obedient, putting her toys and coat away when told.

In contrast, her eight-year-old brother Teddy threw temper tantrums whenever he didn't get his way. By always catering to him, they were overlooking Liddy's needs.

As he grew, Teddy traveled with a gang, drank alcohol regularly, and skipped school. Fights between Teddy and his parents erupted weekly. During these outbursts, Liddy stood in her older brother's shadow, peering around the corner.

Be the voice of the overlooked sibling. What is said but not heard? Shout it out.

PART VI. MAINTAINING OTHER RELATIONSHIPS

1. My Interconnections

Romantic partners, coworkers, bosses, teachers, and friends might have a difficult time dealing with your depressive episodes on an ongoing basis. Unfortunately, they might tire of your moods and not empathize with you. You might be misunderstood and rejected. Other people might end their relationships with you by ending a marriage, breaking off a friendship, or firing you from a job.

Debbie Downer

Debbie was nine when her mother died giving birth to her younger brother. Her father, with five children to raise alone, became an alcoholic. Her father was mean when he drank, often telling his children he wished they'd never been born.

Despite her difficult upbringing, Debbie was very successful. As a young adult, Debbie landed a job in a law firm, where she met her lawyer husband. They moved to a single-family house in the suburbs of Chicago. They had three children. As the saying goes, she had it all.

But Debbie was always depressed. Her husband tried to help her numerous times, but she rejected his attempts. He spoke to her doctors, family, and friends.

Eventually her husband gave up, developed interests without her, and moved on with his life. Her children grew up and moved away. Her friends, who called her "Debbie Downer," dropped her. Too despondent to recognize her depression, Debbie was now alone.

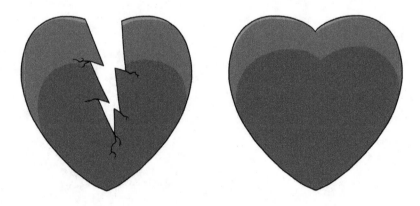

Did depressive episodes ever cause you to alienate family relationships, break up a romantic relationship, or lose friendships?

If so, write the names of the people in the broken heart. Who means the most to you?

Write their names in the intact heart. Indicate how depression affects you and your relationships.

How can those who are significant in your life help you?

Part VII. Healing

1. My Practice of Mindfulness

Depressed people often ignore their health. When you're depressed, taking care of yourself seems like the last thing you want to do. But more than ever, when you're depressed, you need to pay extra attention to your whole being, including your physical, emotional, cognitive, and spiritual health. When we feel healthy, we have more to give to others.

In recent years, scientists have found a correlation between physical health and mindfulness. During depressive episodes, we replay past events and/or perceive a negative outlook for the future. Mindfulness is a therapeutic technique that can be helpful during these occurrences.

Mindfulness involves achieving a mental state by simultaneously focusing on the present moment and acknowledging and accepting one's feelings, thoughts, and bodily sensations. Mindfulness teaches you to stay in the here and now, stop obsessing on the past or worrying about might what happen, and relinquish any judgments for yourself or others.

Living a life without judgment is an important aspect of practicing mindfulness.

Last Judgment

Francis who was a trial court judge, not only passed judgment in his courtroom, but he harshly judged and criticized all the people in his personal life. He drove his wife, children, friends, and many colleagues away.

One day a homeless man appeared in his courtroom. He was being prosecuted for sleeping on private property because he hadn't anywhere to live.

As the homeless man stood before him, Francis demanded, "Why don't you have people in your life to help you?"

The homeless man, who was wiser than Francis suspected, replied, "I ask you, Your Honor, why don't you have people in your life to help you?"

Shocked, Francis lifted his gavel, then stopped. This homeless man was right. Francis left the courtroom and never returned.

Are you judgmental?

About what or whom? List them.

Have you noticed that criticism comes full circle?

2. MY PRACTICE OF GRATITUDE

Studies show that being grateful can boost your health, improve your relationships, make you more empathetic and understanding, help you sleep, and enhance your overall mental outlook.

Miserable Marnack the Monk

Marnack the monk mocked the birds for singing. He cursed the trees for providing all the wood he had to chop. He scolded the river for offering its endless supply of water, which he had to carry in buckets back to the monastery for many miles.

One day Marnack was chopping a tree, and he cut a deep wound in his leg. Filled with rage, he dropped to his knees, crying loudly. There was no one to help him. He had to rely on himself. He had to become mindful in saving his own life.

He carved crutches and a splint out of wood. He hobbled to the river and drank water. By listening to the birds sing, he stayed calm. For the first time, his mind became peaceful. After returning safely to the monastery, Marnack pledged to live a life free of anger.

Identify areas of your life that may seem monotonous or grinding to you. Imagine how grateful you feel that you have this boring life.

Make a gratitude list and watch it grow throughout the years.

Repeat a mantra that you like or try this one.

A quiet place, a quiet mind,
a peaceful space I must resign,
each peaceful step, each grateful step.

3. MY PRACTICE OF AWARENESS

We are all guilty of losing awareness. When it happens, it's as though someone switched the brain to cruise control. We become unconscious and begin to criticize, judge, shame, abandon, and cause others pain.

Hilda and the Birds

Hilda wailed about the way her life had turned out. She complained about her dead husband, whom she called a fool for leaving her alone. She berated her children, who never came to see her. She condemned her former place of employment, a factory where she had fallen, injuring her back so that she suffered chronic pain. Each morning she sat by her window, wishing to die.

One morning she noticed a pair of goldfinches pecking at her window.

"Maybe they are trying to communicate with me," she thought.

The next day Hilda tripped, fell to the floor, and passed out. While unconscious, Hilda dreamed of the birds. They told her to accept her life; the time would come when she would understand her destiny. When she awoke, she saw the goldfinches outside her window.

"I understand," she told them. "You are right."

What would you become mindful and aware of if the birds pecked at your window?

Do you accept your life and everything in it?

Why or why not?

4. MY STRESSES

People know they should manage stress. Some people don't understand how much stress contributes to depression, especially if the stress is prolonged.

We become so busy juggling our days. Stress sometimes seeps into our lives and worsens our depression.

The Juggler

Jared the juggler knew that his family complained because he took on too many challenges. When the king put forth the latest challenge, Jared accepted another. He wished to win the top prize, a chest filled with gold.

At first Jared had to juggle three balls, then four, then five, all of which he accomplished easily. The king then asked Jared to juggle three fire torches while walking across a wooden beam that straddled a snake pit. Accomplished!

The last feat was the most difficult. The king asked Jared to juggle five fire torches while standing on a floating log in a moat filled with alligators.

As he tossed the torches, Jared suddenly lost his balance. The torches flew from his hands and landed on the king, who flailed wildly and fell into the moat. The alligators swallowed the king.

What activities are you juggling? List them.

How do they impact your family and friends?

What do you lose by juggling too many things at once?

How does all this juggling affect your moods?

What can you do to simplify your life?

5. MY STRAINS

Sometimes it's not until something dire happens that we are forced to stop and pay attention to our lives.

Storms Brewing

Frank worked as a nurse in a nursing home for twenty years. Every day he felt more pressured and exhausted.

He was reprimanded by patronizing supervisors who criticized his efforts. He was taunted by coworkers for following the rules. He constantly worried that the nursing home would be sold and he'd lose his job. He often worked with terminally ill residents, and the smell of death was more than he could endure.

After work, Frank never had time to care for himself. His wife had multiple sclerosis, and his son suffered with severe depression and addiction issues. Even with his medical insurance and salary, Frank had accumulated a mountain of medical bills. Little did Frank realize that the biggest storm was yet to hit.

Finish the story.

Identify the biggest storm that ever hit you.

What stressors have you had?

How did they make you feel?

How did you cope?

Did anyone help you handle the difficulties?

6. MY SPIRIT GUIDES

Nature has a way of guiding us when we become quiet and choose to listen with our hearts. Connecting with nature can lift our mental outlook, our emotions, and our spirits.

The Wild Dog of Costa Rica

After a relationship ended, Isabelle felt lost and forlorn. She took a job in an orphanage in Costa Rica, where the rugged land and diverse wildlife captivated her. In this new country, she hoped to find new meaning in her life.

One afternoon, while Isabelle and a friend were hiking on a mountain, a storm rushed in, bringing heavy fog and rain. The frightened pair became stranded.

Suddenly a dog appeared from out of the clouds, approached them, and wagged his tail. The village residents had warned Isabelle not to befriend the wild dogs of Costa Rica.

But soon the girls realized that the dog wanted them to follow him. With night coming and no other choices, they did. They soon were at the mountain's base and near the safety of the valley. They looked for the dog, but he had disappeared.

When they recounted their story, the townspeople told them the roaming dogs were usually vicious. This dog must have been their spirit guide.

Who or what can become your spirit guides?

Do you depend on guides in your life?

How can spirit guides help you?

7. MY HEALTH

Healthy habits and routines are established when you get adequate sleep, eat nutritiously, exercise regularly, have relaxation time, and take any necessary medications and vitamins.

Other healthy, nonmedical approaches for depression include acupuncture, yoga, massage therapy, mediation, and herbal supplements.

We tend to make excuses that stop us from making our whole being a priority.

Complete the sentences below. Describe your feelings. If you have trouble, ask someone to help you.

I can't manage stress because

My solution is

I don't get enough sleep because

My solution is

I don't exercise consistently because

My solution is

When vitamins are recommended and medicines are prescribed by my doctor, I either don't take them consistently or don't take them at all because

My solution is

I choose not to have personal or relaxation time because

My solution is

When psychotherapy is recommended, I choose not to participate because

My solution is

I don't feel that I have enough positive relationships because

My solution is

PART VIII. TREATMENT OPTIONS

Nowadays, trying to find the best treatment choice for your depression is like tracking your way out of a jungle.

You can start by consulting your primary care physician, who might have suggestions. Primary care physicians can also offer medications, but they do minimal talk therapy.

Other sources of mental health recommendations are through family members and friends.

To determine what kind of treatment you might need, it's important to ask yourself questions: Do I think I need medication? Do I think I might have a biological or genetic component to depression? Has a traumatic event caused my depression? Would exploring my feelings in a setting where other people are doing the same be helpful for me?

Other criteria to help determine your choices are the availability of the mental health practitioner and method choices. Sometimes the most important benchmark of choice is that the relationship between you and your mental health practitioner is trusting, nonjudgmental, and just feels right.

On the following pages, describe any experience you've had seeking help for your depression from the following.

1. MY PSYCHIATRIST

A psychiatrist is a medical doctor specializing in the diagnosis and treatment of mental illness. They are able to prescribe medicine. Psychiatrists have an understanding of the biological and genetic factors and the chemistry of the brain. They try to determine what medications best fit or target the symptoms that a patient reports.

2. MY NEUROLOGIST

A neurologist is a medical doctor specializing in the anatomy, functions, and organic disorders of the body's nervous system. They treat illnesses affecting the brain, spinal cord, and nerves. Depression is often caused by a head injury that has caused trauma to the brain. Neurologists are also able to prescribe medicine.

3. MY PSYCHOLOGIST, COUNSELOR, SOCIAL WORKER, FAMILY THERAPIST, OR MARITAL THERAPIST

A psychologist has a doctoral degree in psychology, the study of the mind and human behavior. They are trained to look closely at a person's behavior. Unlike psychiatrists and neurologists, most are not able to prescribe medicine; however, some psychologists, with additional training and under certain restrictions, may be licensed to do so. Certain states offer this privilege.

Counselors, social workers, and marital therapists are mental health workers who have a master's or doctorate degree and are trained to treat individuals, families, and groups who are trying to overcome mental illness and emotional or behavioral problems.

4. MY CLERGY

Priests, ministers, rabbis, brothers, sisters, or other members of religious communities can offer counseling services and be a wonderful source of support.

5. MY INTENSIVE OR INPATIENT CARE

Severe depression may require inpatient treatment or hospitalization. Residential treatment programs offer twenty-four-hour supervision and intensive, comprehensive support. There are also day treatment and intensive outpatient programs available that offer maximum care and help.

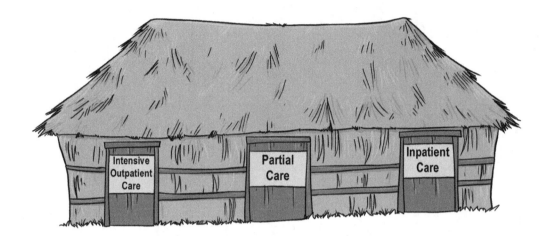

IX. Support Systems

1. My Support Groups

One of the keys to getting well and taking care of yourself is building and maintaining strong support systems. Depression can worsen if you isolate yourself and try to deal with depression alone.

When you are dealing with depression, mental improvement and emotional healing are fostered when you maintain healthy connections with people.

Support system members can be friends, family members, neighbors, and coworkers. Other networks are those that share an involvement in mental health care, such as therapists, group therapy practices, online groups, school clubs, nonprofit organizations, and governmental agencies.

A few established organizations include the National Association on Mental Illness (www.nam.org); Depression Bipolar Support Alliance (www.dballiance.org); American Psychological Association (www.apa.org); and the National Institute of Mental Health (www.nimh.nih.gov).

The Deep Hole

When the wooden plank split apart, five hikers tumbled ten feet into an old mineshaft. With no cell phone reception and no other hikers for miles, the group became dismayed. They then tried grabbing onto tree roots to hoist themselves out. When that failed, they tied clothing together in a chain and tossed it up in hopes of their clothing chain catching onto a branch. That didn't work either. As night descended, the weary hikers huddled under a hut of sticks and backpacks.

The next day their plight still seemed hopeless until one hiker suggested that the group form a human chain and stand on each other's shoulders. The hiker on top of the human chain climbed out of the hole successfully. He secured a rope to a tree, and each hiker ascended from the mineshaft.

When time came for the last hiker to vacate the hole, he decided not to leave. You are that person.

What stops you from wanting help? Searching deep inside yourself, write a note to your inner voice asking for help.

PART X. LESSONS OF DEPRESSION

1. My Authentic Self

Again and again, we find ourselves having to accept situations that seem especially impossible, such as the end of a relationship, the death of a loved one, the aging of ourselves or others, the loss of a job, or financial despair.

When you affirm your authentic self, your mind and body become alive and illuminated. Affirming your true self means taking action to meet your needs, expressing who you really are, and thinking good thoughts about yourself.

Depression might feel like alienation from others. More importantly, however, depression alienates you from your deeper self. You need to reclaim yourself for you.

Depression appears when you feel locked in place and believe there is no way out. If you ask for help or guidance, you can find your way out and start on the path to your authentic self.

Authentic Love Will Find Its Way

Victoria was the principal of a therapeutic boarding school. Only five feet tall, Victoria could be intimidating, yet she was also revered and respected by her students. She controlled them through authentic love peppered with honesty, humbling the most defiant kids and bringing them to their knees.

Seventeen-year-old Billy was one of those kids. He fiercely argued and blamed others, never taking responsibility for his problems.

One day Billy slipped under the fence and ran away. He stole an innertube and paddles from the garage and jumped into the river.

After floating alone for hours, Billy began to cry, feeling rejected, unwanted, and abandoned. Through his tears, he heard his name being called. On the river's bank, he saw a familiar face.

"Billy, there is no place to run or hide from the truth of the matter," said Victoria, with outstretched arms.

Billy knew that Victoria was right. He paddled to the shore, and when he stepped onto the ground, Victoria hugged him tightly.

On their ride back to school, Billy asked Victoria, "How did you know where I was?"

Victoria said, "Both truth and love find their way." For the first time, Billy didn't argue.

Who do you blame?

What do you defend yourself against?

What rules do you break?

What do you run from?

Who will accept you?

Who will love you?

Who do you authentically trust?

Who loves you authentically?

2. MY STORY

We all encounter depression in our lifetimes. It can be difficult to make sense of all the conflicts, challenges, and pain in our lives. For now, be open to the lessons of depression. Lessons are revealed to us as we experience life in its fullness. Every emotion we feel guides us to higher levels of consciousness and spiritual awakening.

My hope is that you have discovered the ***truth of the matter*** by unraveling the causes of your depression. Having a better understanding of depression, learning strategies to cope with depression, and being aware of available resources will allow you to take action in helping yourself. When you free yourself from family conflicts and any anger toward others, you embrace the ***heart of the matter*** and lessen or alleviate your depression.

The richness of life includes times of discomfort and experiences of depression. Your depression will imprint new lessons as the authentic you emerges. The goal is that depression will no longer be your enemy or hold you hostage in emotional despair. Your soul will be free to experience the richness of life.

From here, it's up to you to move on and stay committed to healing yourself.

Go back to the beginning of this journal and review it in its entirety. Take notice of which questions you might have skipped. Perhaps now you can answer them. If not, wait until the answers are revealed to you.

Think back on the earlier you and your story.

This last story is the story that will reflect your life from this moment on.

What positive changes have occurred through struggles you might have experienced?

Who did you meet and what relationships have you formed?

In conclusion, the door is open for you to begin to think optimistically, feel better, and connect with your inner sanctum. This is the essence of ***The Mind, Heart, and Soul of Depression.***

Printed in the United States
By Bookmasters